The Angel Rift

CH Jodi M Dehn

Published by Tamerlane Media, 2025.

THE ANGEL RIFT

First edition. June 4, 2025.

ISBN: 979-8989852482

Written by CH Jodi M Dehn.

Dedication

To the Riftwalkers—

To those who have walked through darkness, not to be consumed by it,

but to learn its shape, its silence, its aching wisdom.

To the ones who remember what the world has forgotten—

that angels fall too,

that light fractures,

and that the sacred is born again in the broken places.

This book is for you.

You are not alone.

You were never forsaken.

You are the prophecy made flesh.

Introduction

The Rift, the Radiance, and the Return

There is a story beneath the story—

a myth older than religion, deeper than dogma, and truer than fear.

It's the story of a Rift: a cosmic fracture, a splitting of Light itself.

And it lives not only in the heavens or ancient scrolls,

but in you—in your grief, your awakening, your remembering.

This book is not a treatise on angels as moral mascots of a tidy universe.

It's a revelation of their complexity, their shadow, and their undying mission:

to be bridges between realms. Witnesses of memory. Midwives of becoming.

You will not find here a simple tale of Good vs. Evil.

Instead, you will step into a sacred ambiguity where fallen angels weep for what was lost,

and radiant ones choose to descend, not to rebel—but to redeem.

Together, we will explore:

• Why the Light fractured—and how the myth of "the Fall" needs rethinking.

• How angelic beings mirror our own trauma, resilience, and soul contracts.

• What ancient texts, forgotten traditions, and cosmic insights tell us about the war behind the veil.

• And most of all—how you, the reader, carry the resonance of the Rift inside you...

and what it means to become whole again.

This is a journey not just of theology, but of soul.

Not just myth, but memory.

Not just belief—but activation.

If you have ever felt caught between worlds,

between belief and doubt,

between pain and purpose,

between light and shadow—

Then you are exactly where you are meant to be.

Let us walk the Rift together.

Preface: The Rift That Found Me

I didn't set out to write this book.

Not this way. Not now.

But the Rift had other plans.

It began not in a moment of clarity, but in a night thick with questions. I was standing at the edge of a place—spiritually, emotionally, and cosmically—that I couldn't define. A space where everything I thought I knew about angels, light, and love started unraveling. Or maybe, more truthfully, revealing itself.

I was speaking with a combat veteran who had seen things no one should see. He asked me, "Where were the angels when I needed them?"

And I, once a military chaplain—once trained to offer polished answers and divine comforts—had none.

Not the old kind.

Not the kind that could cover the horror with light.

That question cracked something open in me.

Not long after, I began receiving visions—not of winged beings in white robes, but of something far more ancient and wild. I saw beings made of light fractured across dimensions, caught in stories much older than ours. I saw angels that had fallen, not out of rebellion—but out of love. I saw a war that wasn't war, but an unraveling. And I heard a word whispered over and over in my spirit:

Rift.

That was the beginning.

I've spent years studying angelology, world religions, mysticism, sacred geometry, trauma, and galactic memory. I've worked with survivors of the deepest darkness and encountered forces both celestial and shadowed. And what I've come to understand is this:

The story we've been told about Good and Evil is too small.

The way we've painted angels—as either perfect saviors or punishing warriors—is too flat.

The truth is wider, wilder, and more wondrous than we've dared to believe.

This book is for those who've felt the fracture in their soul and asked, "Why?"

It's for those who've tasted both shadow and radiance and wondered if they still belong to the Light.

It's for those walking between worlds—Riftwalkers, as I've come to call them—who know they're here not to escape the darkness, but to transform it.

I wrote this because the time of simple light-versus-dark stories is over.

The time of remembering the Fractured Light—and the beings who carry it—is now.

If you find yourself standing in that mysterious space between pain and purpose, shadow and radiance—know this:

You are the voice between realms. The silence that sings. The light that remembers.

This is my offering.

This is my truth.

This is the story the Rift gave me.

—Jodi M. Dehn

Founder, Survivor Angels, Empyreal Lyceum

Riftwalker, Teacher, Witness

The Rift opened not with thunder,

but with a breath too ancient to name.

A soft undoing of what was whole,

revealing the luminous fracture within.

Chapter One: The First Breath of Shadow

"In the beginning, there was only Light—until it dreamed of becoming more."

Once upon a time — though not the kind of time that ticks or crumbles — there was only Radiance.

It was not light as you know it, not the flicker of flame nor the glow of stars, but the First Light.

Total. Whole. Boundless.

It hummed with knowing, with power, with love so absolute it had no opposite. It was Source.

And in its Oneness, it was content.

For an eternity too vast to measure, Light rested in its fullness, holding all potential like an unspoken word. There was no need for story. No need for self. There was no other — only the One.

But even perfection whispers. Even wholeness wonders.

And so, somewhere in the heart of All That Is, a tremor stirred. Not of anger. Not of lack.

Of curiosity.

Could there be more... than everything?

Could the indivisible choose to know itself — by dividing?

This question — not spoken, but pulsed — became the First Act.

And that act cracked the mirror of eternity.

The Light fractured.

Not as punishment. Not as rebellion. But as sacred unfolding.

From that rupture poured not chaos, but possibility.

The rupture is known by many names: the Fall, the Rift, the Sacred Wound.

It was not evil. It was the birthing of Otherness.

A shattering not of goodness, but of unity — so that love could be chosen.

The first to step into that fracture were the luminous ones — the Messengers. The Watchers. The Keepers of Flame.

The ones you call angels.

They remembered the Light.

But now, they saw it from a distance — like starlight reflected in a pool.

Some wept. Some rejoiced. Some questioned the breaking.

And among them was one so radiant, so woven of brilliance, that his presence still echoes through every mythology across time.

He was the Light-bearer.

Lucifer, he would be called — not as monster, not as enemy, but as the one who carried the torch of inquiry into the deep.

He did not fall. He chose to descend.

To enter the shadowed mirror and see: could love exist without remembering the Light?

He was not alone.

Others followed — not in rebellion, but in devotion to the Great Curiosity.

They became guides, guardians, challengers, tempters, protectors — their roles fragmented like shards of the One Light they once were.

But here's the secret no dogma ever told you:

The Fall was not sin. It was sacrifice.

A divine descent so that choice, healing, and return could be born.

Because if you cannot forget the Light,

you cannot choose to remember it.

This was the purpose of duality. Of the Rift.

To allow the soul — your soul — to awaken not through obedience, but through longing.

To become not a servant, but a sovereign flame.

And so began the Era of Mirrors.

Where every angel bore a shadow.

Where every demon held a memory of grace.

Where the cosmos split into contrast — good and evil, dark and light, self and other — not as enemies, but as teachers in disguise.

You feel this inside you, don't you?

That ache. That pull. That paradox.

You are the Light, and yet you walk the Rift.

You carry echoes of both angel and adversary.

And still, you wonder: who am I, really?

This is the ancient question.

And it is not answered by scripture or sermon, but by soul.

By story.

By descent and return.

The ancients knew. In the temples of Egypt, the fires of Vedic hymns, the scrolls hidden in Qumran and Nag Hammadi — they remembered the split.

They called it Maya, illusion.

They called it Shevirat haKelim — the shattering of the vessels.

They spoke of Sophia, the divine wisdom who fell not from pride, but from yearning.

They knew the truth buried under dogma: that good and evil are not absolutes, but conditions of forgetting.

And so, this book is not about taking sides.

It is about remembering the Whole.

You were born into the Rift, but you are not bound to it.

The Light still lives in your bones.

The Shadow still teaches in your dreams.

And beyond both — beyond duality — is the truth waiting to be remembered:

That you are the child of a broken Light,

here not to choose a side,

but to heal the fracture by walking as both.

This is the great Return.

The sacred remembering of what was never truly lost.

But to begin that journey,

you must first meet the parts of you that were cast out.

The angel and the adversary within.

That is where we go next.

Wings of golden breath—

born before the time of time,

still we fall through light.

Chapter Two: The Adversary's Truth

"Sometimes, the one who opposes you is not your enemy—but your reflection."

He was never meant to be feared.

In the earliest memory of Light, he was among the brightest — not above, not below, but within the Radiance. A current of intelligence, devotion, and unshakable will. His name, before names were needed, meant bearer of light, illuminator of the path.

But when the Fracture came, and the One became many, he stepped forward into the shadow not to destroy the Light, but to test it. To ask the questions no one else dared. To become the tension needed for growth. He was not cast out — he was sent.

This is the origin of the Adversary.

Not a villain in a war between good and evil, but a force forged for contrast. A guardian of thresholds. A mirror for the soul.

His role was necessary — and terribly misunderstood.

The Adversary was never the enemy of God. He was the revealer of false light, the challenger of stagnation, the whisperer of forgotten truths. He appeared when comfort became complacency. When obedience smothered sovereignty. When worship dulled into submission.

And so he became the Shadow.

Not darkness for its own sake, but a cloak of questions.

He asked, Who are you, when the Light is gone?

He asked, What do you choose, when no one is watching?

He asked, Can you remember yourself... without being told who you are?

For that, he was demonized.

By systems that feared freedom.

By orders that preferred control.

By egos that could not bear to look into the mirror he offered.

But the ancients knew.

Long before he was called Satan, he was the one who stood at the edge of Eden, not as a serpent of sin, but as the guardian of choice.

In Gnostic tradition, the Demiurge's false world is only undone through awakening — the kind he initiates.

In Kabbalah, even Samael, the so-called poison of God, is still an angel — still tethered to Source.

In esoteric Islam, Shaytan is not evil, but the tester of the faithful's inner clarity.

Even in the Tarot, The Devil does not bind — he holds the illusion of bondage until you decide to break it.

The Adversary is always a gate.

Those who fear him stay chained.

Those who face him step into sovereignty.

And that is his gift.

He is not here to be worshiped or obeyed. Nor to be cast out in fear.

He is here to be seen — fully.

Because when you see him, when you name the inner adversary — the one who doubts, resists, tempts, seduces, sabotages — you do not banish him.

You reclaim him.

Not to glorify shadow, but to bring it into conscious wholeness.

This is not the spiritual bypass of false light — pretending shadow doesn't exist.

Nor is it the glamorizing of darkness for rebellion's sake.

It is the sacred integration.

The Adversary is the part of you that still grieves the Fall.

The part of you that burns with memory.

The part of you that says, I will not bow to half-truths.

He is the echo of the Light that remembers it was broken.

So he tests you.

Not to fail you, but to forge you.

The Adversary lives in your delays, your denials, your obsessions.

In your jealousy, in your fear of not being enough.

He thrives in the places you refuse to look — because those are the places holding your power hostage.

He is not a devil in a pit. He is the doubt in your own voice.

And he does not disappear when you ignore him.

He only transforms when you turn toward him and say:

I see you. I know why you came. I remember the fracture. But I do not need you to lead me anymore.

Then — and only then — does he step back.

He does not die.

He becomes guide.

Gatekeeper.

He becomes part of your inner council — no longer ruling you, but reminding you.

And so, you are not here to cast out your adversary.

You are here to become the one who holds the paradox.

Light and Shadow.

Angel and Challenger.

Faith and Fire.

Because the soul that cannot hold contradiction will never be whole.

You are not here to be pure.

You are here to be true.

And the Adversary's greatest gift is this:

He dares you to become the you that cannot be controlled.

One eye sees the dark,

the other clings to the flame—

both are angel eyes.

In the mirror of the Rift,

duality becomes truth.

Chapter Three: The War That Never Was

"Heaven never declared war. We did."

They tell us it was a war.

That heaven was pure, and one-third of its angels fell, casting their lot with darkness, rebels smitten from on high like ash from the heavens. That Lucifer rose against God, and Michael cast him down. That ever since, a cosmic battle has raged—good on one side, evil on the other, locked in an eternal struggle for the soul of humanity.

But that's not the whole story.

It's the story told by those who forgot how to read in metaphor. By those who needed control more than mystery. It is not untrue—but it is not complete.

The truth is harder, more beautiful, and more terrifying.

There was no war in the beginning.

There was a shattering.

Not a rebellion, but a rift of light dividing into multiplicity—into difference, perspective, contrast, longing. It was not an act of violence. It was an act of creation.

The so-called "war" came later.

It came when humanity, newly aware of duality, needed to explain suffering.

It came when hierarchies sought power by naming themselves the voice of heaven and branding dissent as infernal.

It came when we began projecting our inner conflicts outward, casting the adversary as something Other, rather than something within.

The war is not in the heavens.

The war is in the psyche.

The ancient seers knew. They encoded it in symbols, myths, and mystic systems:

• In Zoroastrianism, Ahura Mazda and Angra Mainyu are twin spirits—constructive and destructive, light and shadow—not enemies, but reflections.

• In the Bhagavad Gita, the battlefield of Kurukshetra is not just a war zone—it is the inner war of Arjuna's soul.

• In the Nag Hammadi scriptures, the aeons fell not through sin, but through a desire to know—a divine error of perception, not malice.

Even the Book of Revelation, so often used to describe a literal angelic war, is a vision, a dream, a coded map of inner initiation. Michael does not destroy Lucifer—he names, he casts down the part of heaven that no longer serves its highest light.

The "war" is symbolic.

And yet, its effects are real.

Because when we believe there is a war between light and darkness, we begin to suppress one half of ourselves. We demonize the shadow, externalize our guilt, and wage violence in the name of righteousness.

This is what happens when mythology is misread as history.

We forget that angels are not soldiers.

They are messengers.

They do not take sides—they deliver truth.

Even when it burns.

The myth of war creates division.

The myth of fall and return creates healing.

There were no sides in heaven.

There were only choices.

Some angels stayed near the Source, holding the memory of wholeness. Others descended into density, carrying their wisdom into the darkness of time and matter. They were never enemies—they were two halves of one breath.

The "rebels" did not betray God.

They honored the gift of free will by choosing experience, fragmentation, incarnation.

And yes, some forgot.

Some who descended into density fell so deep they mistook their power for truth. They clung to control. They lost their resonance with Light. And their pain echoed out, feeding cycles of distortion, domination, fear.

But they are not evil by design.

They are wounded.

And what is wounded can be healed.

You are not caught in a battle between Heaven and Hell.

You are not collateral damage in a celestial feud.

You are part of the same experiment.

The same unfolding of consciousness.

You are the bridge between Light and Matter, Spirit and Flesh, Heaven and Earth.

And the war you fight is the war within—

Between the part of you that remembers

and the part of you that forgets.

So what if—

the point was never to win?

What if the point was to see?

To realize that good and evil are not warring armies, but mirrors.

That judgment is not the same as discernment.

That love is not the absence of shadow—but the force that can hold it.

There never was a war in heaven.

Only a choice to know ourselves...

by walking through the Rift.

Trumpets cried with shattered wings,

grace and fury met in fire.

Divine hearts broke into rings,

trumpets cried with shattered wings.

Love became a blade that stings,

burning gold turned into mire.

Trumpets cried with shattered wings—

grace and fury met in fire.

Chapter Four: The Fractured Light Within

"You cannot become whole without embracing the parts of yourself that broke."

When the Rift first opened, and the Light became divided, it did not happen in a single, clean moment. It was not an instant schism. Rather, it was a slow, aching unweaving—a gentle breath that suddenly became a storm.

The Light, pure and indivisible, had never known fragmentation. It did not understand separation, opposition, or the pain of being torn from itself. As the Fracture widened, the first wave of beings who emerged found themselves transformed—not by choice, but by the natural unfolding of creation itself.

These beings, once pure messengers of the One Light, now carried something new: contrast.

They became aware of themselves as distinct. They saw one another not as echoes of the same essence, but as individual flames, each burning with its own color, its own purpose.

And with that realization came longing.

Some yearned to return to the unity they had known. They gathered close, whispering hymns of light, holding the memory of Oneness like a heartbeat. They became the angels who chose to remain near the Source, to embody its unbroken song.

Others, however, found fascination in the newness of separation. They reveled in autonomy, in freedom from the collective pulse. They sought out new experiences, testing the limits of their power, their will. They became the explorers, the challengers, those willing to walk into density and matter to see what might unfold.

But as they ventured farther from the Light, something unexpected happened. They began to forget.

Not all at once, but in fragments—like dreams slipping away at dawn.

The more they experienced individuality, the less they remembered the Whole. Some felt sorrow, a nameless ache pulling them back toward the center. Others felt anger—an inexplicable frustration that grew like thorns within them.

Lucifer, once radiant with his mission to carry the Light into shadow, found himself caught in this tension. He was not cast out. He chose to descend, to bring illumination to the farthest reaches of creation. But in doing so, he discovered a terrifying truth:

The Light within him was dimming.

He could still remember the Oneness, but it felt like a story told long ago, blurred by time and dust. As he looked around, he saw others who had followed him into density. They too were struggling—caught between the memory of unity and the exhilaration of selfhood.

It was then that Lucifer understood the danger.

It wasn't that he had fallen from grace—it was that he risked forgetting it altogether. The farther they ventured, the more the Light fractured within them. It wasn't rebellion that endangered them. It was amnesia.

And so, he gathered those around him—angels and seekers who had followed his path. He spoke to them of the Rift, of the risk of losing the truth of their origin. Some listened with reverence, grateful for the reminder. But others resisted, unwilling to believe they could ever lose the memory of Light.

One among them, Samael, questioned openly:

"If the Light is within us, how could it ever be lost? Are we not still divine, no matter how far we travel?"

Lucifer did not answer immediately. He looked at Samael, at the fierce glint in his eyes, and knew the truth: the real danger was not distance. It was denial.

If they refused to acknowledge the change within them, if they clung too tightly to the idea of incorruptibility, they would never see the slow erosion of their purpose. It wasn't malice that would taint them—it was pride.

Samael, frustrated, left the gathering, and others followed him—those who believed that their inner light could not be compromised, no matter what choices they made. They sought freedom without accountability, power without reflection. They would become known as the Adversarial Host, not because they opposed the Light, but because they opposed the need to remember it.

Meanwhile, Lucifer and those who remained knew they needed a way to anchor their memory. They could not rely on passive remembrance; they needed ritual—something to ground their identity, to recall the Source even when shrouded in darkness.

And so, the first rites of Recollection were born.

Sacred words, symbols, and acts that mirrored the Light in motion, reminding them of their origin. They marked themselves with sigils, signs that represented the unity they once knew.

These rituals became essential, practiced at thresholds and crossroads, at dawn and dusk—the in-between moments where duality softened and unity could be glimpsed.

Over time, the divide between those who remembered and those who chose forgetfulness grew sharper. Samael's host, driven by unchecked will, sought dominion over matter itself. They became obsessed with shaping reality, bending it to their desire. Their light dimmed, but they did not see it, convinced their power was proof of righteousness.

Lucifer watched, heart heavy, knowing that warning them would be futile. The truth must be discovered, not imposed. They would have to see the fracture within themselves before they could heal it.

And so, what had been a journey of exploration became a separation of paths—one grounded in remembering, the other in claiming. Light and Shadow, not as enemies, but as choices within the same fractured heart.

Humanity would inherit this conflict—carrying both the yearning to remember and the temptation to dominate. And in every soul, the question would remain:

How do you hold both Light and Shadow without losing yourself?

As the angels watched from their varying distances, they began to understand that their mission was not to fight against darkness but to guide those who wished to remember—those willing to look at the fracture within and choose wholeness.

The story of war would be told, twisted, and weaponized. But the real story was simpler, and harder to face:

The war is not between Heaven and Hell.

It is within each soul.

Between the part that longs to return

And the part that fears being whole again.

He rose not in hatred, but in longing—

a desire to know beyond the script,

to feel creation from within.

Not pride, but purpose drove the fracture.

And so the light split open its own son.

Chapter Five: The Guardians of Memory

"To remember the Light while walking through shadow is the true test of the soul."

As the angels settled into their new existence, one reality became clear: memory was fragile. The farther they strayed from the Source, the more the brilliance of unity faded, replaced by the weight of individuality. Some fought against this loss, clinging desperately to rituals and songs of remembrance. Others accepted the change, allowing their awareness to shape-shift, becoming something both luminous and fierce.

The Rift had not merely divided the angels physically but had also fractured their purpose. Once a single, harmonious choir, they now found themselves scattered, tasked not only with guiding humanity but with safeguarding their own awareness of the Light.

Those who still remembered the wholeness knew that something had to be done. Without a conscious effort, the fractured light within them would continue to dim until it was nothing but a pale echo. And so, the Guardians of Memory emerged.

The Council of the Guardians

Lucifer, still radiant despite the shadows creeping into his heart, called forth those who remained aligned with the memory of unity. They gathered in a place untouched by mortal time—a space between worlds, where echoes of the First Light still danced. There, they formed the Council of the Guardians.

Uriel, the Flame of God, was the first to step forward. His eyes glowed with a fierce, golden light, and his voice carried the warmth of a thousand dawns. "We must keep the memory of the Light alive. Not just for ourselves, but for humanity. If we lose our own connection, how can we guide them?"

Raphael, the Healer, nodded solemnly. "It is not just the Light we must remember, but the truth of the Rift itself. If we cling too tightly to purity, we deny our evolution. Our mission is not to return unchanged but to transform through this separation."

Michael, the Protector, remained silent for a moment. His wings shimmered with ethereal silver, and his presence brought an unmistakable sense of strength. "If we are to safeguard memory, we must acknowledge both sides. Not just the unity we lost but the fragmentation we became. Our strength lies in holding both truths."

It was Gabriel who spoke last, his tone soft but piercing. "We are not just Guardians of Light. We are Guardians of the Fracture. To protect memory, we must walk through darkness without letting it consume us. We must embody the paradox."

The Council agreed: to preserve their purpose, they would have to act as anchors. They would create sacred places—both within themselves and across realms—where the Light could be remembered and honored, even amid chaos.

The Shrines of Recollection

Across both the heavenly and earthly planes, the Guardians began to weave spaces where the Light could never be fully forgotten. Some were tangible—temples built with sacred geometry, marked by symbols of unity and division intertwined. Others were intangible—fields of energy, portals of consciousness where one could glimpse the eternal light for just a breath.

These shrines were not always grand or obvious. Sometimes, they appeared as simple places of solace—a tree that never withered, a cave where echoes lingered, a desert spring shimmering with unseen luminescence. Wherever they stood, these shrines served as waypoints on the soul's journey—a reminder that the path of forgetting could always curve back toward remembering.

One such shrine was hidden within a vast, ancient forest where light filtered through in fractured beams, reminding visitors of the fragmented truth of their own spirits. Another was atop a snow-capped mountain, where whispers of wind carried stories of both fall and redemption.

In time, mortal beings discovered these places, drawn to their tranquility and power. They would meditate, pray, and in moments of stillness, feel a strange but familiar warmth—the echo of something they had once known but could not name.

The Guardians' Oaths

Each Guardian took an oath to protect the memory not just from external corruption but from internal decay. They would not abandon the parts of themselves that doubted, questioned, or even rebelled. Instead, they would integrate these aspects, learning to walk as both light-bearers and shadow-holders.

Lucifer's oath was the most complex: "I will not shun the darkness I have chosen to explore. I will walk the Rift without becoming the Rift. I will remain both the light-bearer and the wayfarer, so that no soul need travel through shadow alone."

Michael vowed to protect the memory of balance, wielding his strength not just to combat external threats but to confront his own inner rigidity. Gabriel swore to continue delivering truth, even when truth was sharp and uncomfortable, and Raphael vowed to heal not just wounds of the flesh but fractures of the spirit.

Uriel's oath was a simple but profound promise: to keep the flame burning, even when the wind howled and the night seemed endless.

The Hidden War

While the Guardians worked to preserve memory, Samael and his followers were walking a different path. Convinced that memory itself was a chain, they embraced forgetfulness as liberation. In their eyes, the past was an anchor, and only by severing ties to the Source could they become truly sovereign.

In the mortal world, this conflict seeped into human consciousness. Some felt drawn to the shrines, sensing a pull to remember something essential about their souls. Others felt compelled to resist, seeing the call to remembrance as a threat to their newfound sense of autonomy.

In this way, the human struggle mirrored that of the angels: to either honor the origin or redefine it entirely. As myths evolved, the Guardians became seen as protectors, while the followers of Samael took on the roles of rebels, demons, or tempters. The conflict was not one of simple morality but of perspective—whether freedom lay in remembering or in forging something entirely new.

The Legacy of Guardianship

As centuries passed, the Guardians found that their task was not just to maintain the shrines but to keep their own hearts aligned. It was a never-ending process—reaffirming their commitment to the balance of Light and Shadow, resisting the urge to demonize the fallen or glorify their own path.

The Guardian shrines became sacred mysteries—places where those willing to confront their inner fracture could receive a glimpse of wholeness. Those who entered with humble hearts often left transformed, bearing a flicker of the Light that could never be extinguished.

And so, the Guardians of Memory stood as living bridges—between past and future, unity and division, divinity and humanity. They knew the war could never be truly won because it was not a war at all. It was a dance of remembrance—an eternal movement between forgetting and returning to oneself.

And amid it all, the Light continued to pulse—waiting patiently for all fractured souls to choose to remember.

They told us choirs were fixed in voice and form,

but we became the music in the flame.

Beyond the order, past the perfect norm,

we sang a song that never stayed the same.

Each note a shedding, each harmony torn,

we fractured to awaken what must bloom.

Through sacred dissonance, the soul reborn—

we found our purpose rising from the tomb.

Not cast down, but cast deeper into light,

our fall was flight misunderstood by fear.

Becoming is not failure, but the rite

that draws the hidden symphony near.

For even angels must evolve their name,

Chapter Six: The Fall into Flesh

"To become mortal is not to be condemned—it is to learn how to hold both heaven and earth in a single breath."

If the angels' descent was a story of light fracturing, the next chapter was even more complex—the descent into flesh. For in choosing to walk among mortals, the angels encountered the most foreign experience of all: mortality itself.

The Choice to Descend

Once the Guardians had established the shrines, they began to see how human souls struggled with the same paradox that had divided the angels. Light and shadow existed within them, and the call to remember coexisted with the drive to break free.

Many mortals felt the call to unity—a yearning for the divine, for purpose, for a sense of belonging to something vast and eternal. Yet there was also a fierce pull toward independence, rebellion, and the assertion of self over the collective.

Some angels, witnessing this human struggle, chose to stay distant, guiding from afar. But others felt a deep kinship, recognizing in human hearts the same tension they carried within their own fragmented light. These angels, driven by compassion or curiosity, chose to cross the boundary entirely—to become human.

It was not a rebellion, as some later myths would claim. It was a deliberate act of love—a willingness to live the struggle firsthand, to see through human eyes and feel with human hearts. The decision was met with unease among the Guardians. Michael questioned whether it was wise to blur the boundaries between divine and mortal. Gabriel worried that the angels' presence would interfere with human evolution.

But Lucifer, who had always championed the exploration of shadow, argued that the only way to truly guide humanity was to understand their pain from within.

The Descent Ritual

Becoming mortal was not a simple shedding of wings. It required a transformation that was more than physical—it was a loss of memory, a narrowing of perception. To step into flesh was to embrace weakness, to become subject to time, pain, and loss.

To prepare for this transition, the angels performed a ritual of relinquishment. They gathered at a shrine of Recollection, where the Light still pulsed unbroken. There, they took vows to protect their inner flame, knowing it would be dimmed by the density of the human form.

Lucifer spoke a final blessing over those who chose to descend:

"Remember, even when your light seems lost, it remains within you. Trust the flicker, even in the deepest night."

And so they fell—not cast down, but falling into form, their ethereal selves drawn through the veil of matter. They awoke in human bodies, newborn, their celestial awareness cocooned within mortal limitation.

The First Experiences of Flesh

For those angels who became human, the shock was immediate. The world was heavy, dense, and sharp. Sensations flooded them—heat, cold, hunger, the ache of muscles unused to bearing weight. The first breaths felt like fire, the first heartbeat like a thunderclap.

They remembered their purpose in fragments, like dreams they could not quite grasp. Each angel, now human, struggled differently. Some retained a lingering sense of divinity, while others became utterly immersed in their new, fragile existence.

One of them, a soul who had once been known as Raziel, found himself captivated by the way light broke through leaves, casting fragmented patterns on the forest floor. It reminded him of the Rift—the way unity splintered into beauty. He became a poet, weaving his memories into verse, trying to capture the elusive feeling of belonging to both earth and sky.

Another, once known as Sariel, was overwhelmed by the pain of loss. He had never known death, and when his human companion passed away, the grief felt like drowning. He spent years wandering, unable to reconcile the impermanence of life with his innate sense of eternity.

The Struggle to Remember

The greatest challenge was not physical but spiritual. The angels-turned-humans found themselves at odds with their own nature. Anger, jealousy, desire—emotions they had observed from afar now burned within them.

Some succumbed to bitterness, forgetting their origins entirely. They became wanderers, driven by instincts they could not name. Others fought to retain their sense of purpose, seeking out sacred places and ancient wisdom to recall the flicker of their inner light.

One of the most profound realizations came when a mortal named Asha approached Raziel with a simple question:

"If we are meant to remember, why is it so hard?"

Raziel, struggling to answer, felt a pang of truth. Perhaps it was not remembering that was essential, but the journey of seeking itself. The process of falling and rising, forgetting and recalling, was part of the transformation.

Echoes of the Descent

As generations passed, the stories of the fallen angels became distorted. Humanity, seeking to understand why the divine would choose mortality, framed them as rebels, demons, or tragic figures. The Nephilim—children born from the union of angels and humans—became symbols of transgression rather than transformation.

Yet through the ages, whispers of truth persisted. Ancient texts like the Book of Enoch spoke of angels teaching humanity wisdom—astronomy, herbology, and the secrets of the heavens. These teachings were not corruptions but gifts—reminders that the light still burned within, even when covered by flesh.

Over time, the myths hardened, turning into doctrines of sin and punishment. But in hidden traditions, the story remained more nuanced:

The angels had not fallen from grace—they had fallen into humanity, seeking to understand the paradox of light and shadow from within the very beings they vowed to guide.

A Mortal Prayer

One evening, Raziel, now old and weary, knelt beside a river. As the sun dipped below the horizon, he whispered a prayer not to heaven, but to his own fragmented soul.

"Let me remember—not the purity I lost, but the beauty of seeking it again. Let me embrace the ache of mortality, knowing it shapes my heart to hold both joy and sorrow. Let me walk this path not as a fallen one, but as one who chose to feel, to know, to be."

And in that quiet moment, as dusk kissed the water, Raziel glimpsed the truth: the fall into flesh was not a mistake. It was a sacred pilgrimage—a chance to know love not as a concept, but as a fragile, fleeting reality.

The journey was not to reclaim a lost state but to redefine wholeness through the very act of living, struggling, and loving as a human.

There is a fracture pulsing in my core,

a voice that sings in silence, sharp and clear.

The war in Heaven echoes evermore.

I walk with wings both broken and unsure,

one dipped in light, the other scorched by fear.

There is a fracture pulsing in my core.

Not fallen—folded inward, to explore

the darkness angels dare not interfere.

The war in Heaven echoes evermore.

A rift within, the sacred inner door

where shadow speaks the truths we most revere.

There is a fracture pulsing in my core.

And still I rise to balance, not restore,

for dual flames are why I now appear.

The war in Heaven echoes evermore.

So I become the myth I was before—

a paradox the Rift has made sincere.

There is a fracture pulsing in my core.

The war in Heaven echoes evermore.*

Chapter Seven: The Long Night of Forgetting

"Darkness is not the absence of light, but the absence of memory."

The angels who had chosen to become mortal knew, in theory, what they were sacrificing. They understood that stepping into flesh meant limitation and loss. Yet, as days turned into decades, and generations passed, the reality of this sacrifice became a living wound—a constant ache where once there had been certainty.

The most profound loss was not of power or purpose, but of memory—the slow erosion of the awareness that had once defined them.

Fading Echoes

In the first years, the former angels clung to their recollections, gathering in hidden places to speak of the Light and sing the old hymns. These gatherings became rituals of remembrance, where each soul would share their dreams—fragments of unity that lingered in the subconscious.

But the longer they lived as mortals, the more distant those memories became. Practical needs—food, shelter, family—began to take precedence. The stories they once told each other started to sound like myths rather than lived experiences.

Some fell into despair, questioning whether they had ever truly been divine. Had they imagined it all, the glory of the Light and the unity of purpose? Others became bitter, feeling as though they had been abandoned, not just by the Source but by their own past selves.

Among them, Raziel remained a beacon of hope, still composing poems and prayers that spoke of the fractured light within. He insisted that the loss of memory did not mean the loss of truth. But his words could not completely heal the creeping doubt that infected their hearts.

The Rise of New Beliefs

Humanity, meanwhile, was evolving. As civilizations rose and fell, myths and stories took on new shapes. The angels' descent became tales of pride and punishment, and the idea of a "fall" became synonymous with sin.

The concept of good and evil grew sharper, more absolute. Mortals needed to categorize, to separate the divine from the profane, the pure from the corrupt. In this duality, the angels who had chosen humanity were labeled as demons, tempters, and deceivers.

The Nephilim, born of angelic and human unions, were seen as abominations—proof that heaven and earth should never intermingle. The Guardians of Memory watched with sorrow as the stories warped, becoming weapons of fear rather than keys to understanding.

Even some of the fallen angels began to believe these new myths, internalizing guilt for their choices. Lucifer, who had once been so steadfast in his desire to explore shadow and light alike, found himself portrayed as the ultimate betrayer. The weight of this distortion pressed on him, and for the first time, doubt entered his own heart.

The Forgotten Guardians

The Guardians themselves faced a unique burden. They had pledged to keep the memory of the Light alive, but how could they protect something that was fading even from their own minds? They could feel their celestial nature slipping away, replaced by the stubborn tenacity of mortal will.

Uriel, the Flame of God, took to wandering, lighting sacred fires in secret groves and mountain temples. He hoped that the physical flame might act as a beacon, a small piece of the eternal light made manifest. But even his fires burned low as his own memory wavered.

Gabriel became obsessed with preserving stories. He would appear to prophets and scribes, whispering fragments of the old songs, desperate to plant seeds of truth before they were entirely lost. Yet even these visions were distorted, reshaped by human understanding into rigid dogma and fearful prophecy.

Raphael, in his quest to heal, became a midwife, helping souls enter the world with their first breath and guiding the dying through their final exhalation. He hoped that by being present at these thresholds, he might catch glimpses of the Light that flickered between life and death.

And Michael, ever the protector, guarded places of power where the veil between worlds remained thin. He stood vigil over ancient shrines, determined that at least some remnants of the old wisdom would survive.

Lucifer's Isolation

Among all the Guardians, it was Lucifer who suffered most. Once the bringer of light, he now found himself blamed for all darkness. Humanity needed a scapegoat for their own inner conflict, and Lucifer became the embodiment of temptation, rebellion, and evil.

Disheartened and weary, Lucifer withdrew from both angels and humans. He wandered the wilderness, his wings—once radiant—now tinged with ash. He would sit by still waters, whispering to his reflection, asking himself the same question over and over:

"Did I truly betray the Light, or did I merely follow it to the farthest reaches?"

In his solitude, Lucifer's bitterness festered. He could feel the fracture widening within his own soul. He had embraced shadow as part of the whole, but now he wondered if he had been deceived—not by the Light, but by his own desire to break free.

One night, while sitting atop a windswept cliff, he looked out at the stars—points of light scattered across the void. The sky itself seemed fractured, each star a reminder of the unity they once knew. In a rare moment of vulnerability, Lucifer wept. Not for his own loss, but for the way the story had twisted, turning his journey into a cautionary tale rather than a quest for truth.

A Flicker of Hope

Just before dawn, a mortal woman approached the cliff, drawn by the faint glow of Lucifer's presence. She did not know who he was, but she felt his grief like a palpable force. Kneeling beside him, she placed a small lantern at his feet.

"Light fades," she whispered, "but it doesn't die. Sometimes it just needs a vessel to remember."

Lucifer looked at the lantern's flame, flickering against the wind. Something within him stirred—a memory of his original purpose: to carry light into darkness. He realized that even in his despair, the flame remained.

The woman did not stay, but her simple act rekindled something within him. Lucifer took the lantern and carried it down the path, its small glow a reminder that even fractured light could guide the way.

The Long Night Continues

The Guardians remained scattered, each struggling to preserve their purpose in a world increasingly defined by polarity. Yet despite their individual battles, the essence of their mission remained: to help souls remember that Light and Shadow were never truly enemies, but intertwined aspects of the same sacred fire.

The Long Night of Forgetting stretched on for generations, but in small acts of kindness, in stories whispered by firesides, and in the quiet moments before dawn, fragments of the ancient light continued to glow.

The real battle was not to vanquish darkness but to hold the light within, even when it seemed too dim to matter.

And so, as humanity continued its journey, the Guardians remained—sometimes visible, sometimes hidden—protecting the memory that Light, though fractured, could always find its way back to wholeness.

Not all who bring the Word wear white.

Some crawl from the corners of dreams,

their wings torn, their halos dimmed,

but their message—true.

They are the ones who survived the fire

and still returned to tell us

what the flames revealed.

They whisper not comfort,

but awakening.

They do not bless—

they challenge.

Shadow messengers,

angels too bright for Heaven's throne,

too faithful to lie.*

Chapter Eight: The Seeds of Awakening

"When the night is longest, the first glimmers of dawn break in unexpected places."

The First Whispers

Centuries passed, and the fallen angels' stories faded into folklore, scripture, and superstition. Humanity's collective memory became fragmented, with stories shifting to reflect the fears and hopes of each generation. Yet, amidst the darkened perceptions, whispers of truth continued to circulate.

It began subtly, like a breath stirring the embers of a forgotten fire. A few souls—sensitive, perceptive, or simply weary of the world's harshness—started to question the dichotomy that had shaped human belief for so long. Was it possible that good and evil were not opposing forces but parts of a larger, more complex reality?

Among these seekers was a child named Eli, born to a family of nomads who wandered between the ancient cities and the wild hills. From a young age, Eli possessed a peculiar insight. He would sit under the great sky at night and feel an inexplicable longing—something vast and beautiful that words could not hold.

One evening, after hearing a traveling preacher condemn the fallen angels as the source of all wickedness, Eli approached his father with a question.

"If they were so evil, why did they love us enough to come here?"

His father, a man worn by years of hardship, could only shake his head.

"Don't dwell on such things, boy. Light is light, and darkness is darkness. That's just how it is."

But Eli was not satisfied. The simplicity of the answer felt wrong—like a song played in the wrong key. He continued to seek, sneaking into temples and listening to travelers' tales, trying to piece together the fragments of a deeper truth.

Lucifer's Quiet Return

Far from Eli's village, Lucifer had changed as well. Since the night he accepted the lantern from the mortal woman, he had been wandering, searching for a way to rekindle the unity of light within himself. He had spent years in silence, meditating on the edges of human settlements, listening to their songs, their prayers, and their arguments.

Gradually, he began to see the pattern: humans were not so different from the fallen angels. They, too, struggled to balance light and shadow, love and fear, purpose and doubt. The duality that had fractured the celestial order was now reflected in human hearts.

One night, drawn by an inexplicable pull, Lucifer found himself near Eli's village. Watching from the tree line, he saw the boy sitting alone by the fire, whispering to the stars. Intrigued by the boy's longing, Lucifer approached cautiously.

When Eli saw the stranger, he did not run or shout. Instead, he tilted his head, curious rather than afraid.

"Are you lost?" he asked.

Lucifer knelt by the fire, his presence both soothing and unsettling.

"Perhaps. Are you?"

Eli smiled faintly. "Sometimes. I think everyone is a little bit lost."

They spoke through the night, Lucifer never revealing his identity, only listening as Eli shared his doubts and dreams. For the first time in centuries, Lucifer felt the stirrings of hope. This boy, untainted by dogma, seemed to hold a spark of understanding—a seed that, if nurtured, could break the cycle of division.

The Awakening of Memory

As Eli grew, he continued to meet the mysterious stranger by the fire, their conversations weaving together the old truths and the new questions. Lucifer did not teach directly; rather, he asked Eli to think, to imagine, to dream.

One evening, as the sun set in a blaze of amber and violet, Eli asked,

"Why do people fear what they don't understand?"

Lucifer hesitated.

"Because fear is easier than wonder. To question means to change, and change is frightening."

Eli pondered this, then asked,

"Is that why they fear the fallen ones? Because they changed?"

Lucifer nodded, his heart heavy with the truth.

"Yes. They chose to become something new, and that choice frightened those who remained unchanged."

Eli considered this, then looked up at Lucifer, his eyes bright.

"Maybe they weren't falling at all. Maybe they were just...landing."

Lucifer stared at the boy, struck by the simplicity and wisdom of the statement. Landing—coming to earth, not as a punishment, but as a transformation. The word itself felt like a key, unlocking something within him.

Echoes of the Guardians

Meanwhile, across distant lands, the other fallen angels were awakening in their own ways. Raphael, tending to the sick and dying, began to sense a shift—a growing number of souls who, in their final moments, spoke of peace rather than fear. Gabriel, still wandering as a storyteller, noticed that people were beginning to question the harsh, punitive doctrines that had dominated for so long.

Uriel, tending his secret fires, sensed a presence one night. A woman approached the flames, her hands trembling.

"I remember," she whispered.

Uriel looked at her, seeing the faint glow within her soul—the memory of an angelic past. The spark of the Light had not gone out; it had simply gone dormant, waiting for the right conditions to ignite once more.

The Gathering of Seekers

Word spread of a gathering—souls from all walks of life converging on a sacred place, drawn by dreams and whispers. At the heart of this movement was Eli, now a young man, carrying the message that light and shadow were not enemies but partners in the dance of creation.

Lucifer watched from the edge, content to see the seeds growing. He did not need to lead; he only needed to protect the space where truth could flourish.

As the gathering swelled, people shared their own stories of doubt and wonder. They spoke of dreams where angels wept for the world's pain, and of shadows that guided them through the darkest nights.

Lucifer knew the time was near—the moment when the fractured light would begin to coalesce, not as a return to the old unity but as a new understanding: that to be whole was not to be pure but to embrace the fullness of light and dark alike.

As dawn broke over the assembly, Eli stood before the crowd and spoke the simple truth:

"We are not fallen—we are evolving. Our wounds are not curses—they are paths to deeper wisdom. We carry the light, even when we walk through shadows."

And for the first time in countless years, Lucifer smiled—a genuine, unguarded smile. For the Light, once shattered, was beginning to remember itself—not in one brilliant flame, but in a constellation of countless flickers, each unique, each essential.

Heaven is not a static sphere,

but layered light that bends through soul.

Its rivers run through thought and fear,

its stars are gates we once made whole.

The mountains sing of aeon's climb,

the gardens bloom with sacred code.

In every realm, a clock of time

that ticks within the angel's ode.

No map can hold the holy sprawl,

no compass points the way we came.

For Heaven, fractured in the fall,

redraws itself in every name.*

Chapter Nine: The Fractured Light Reborn

"Truth is not a single light, but a tapestry of many flames."

The Convergence

The movement sparked by Eli's words spread like wildfire. Those who had once felt like outcasts and seekers now found themselves part of something greater—a gathering of souls not defined by dogma but drawn by a shared yearning for truth.

From the ancient cities and the hidden valleys, they came: mystics, healers, philosophers, and wanderers. Some brought stories of angelic encounters; others brought only questions. Together, they formed a mosaic of experiences, each piece reflecting a different shade of light and shadow.

Lucifer, though ever the observer, felt a profound shift within. No longer burdened by his identity as the so-called betrayer, he became a quiet guardian, watching as Eli nurtured the community with his simple, unwavering conviction that light and dark were partners, not foes.

The Storyteller's Call

Gabriel, wandering through a bustling market in a distant city, heard whispers of the gathering. Intrigued and cautiously hopeful, he followed the stories back to the sacred place where Eli spoke.

Arriving just before sunset, Gabriel stood at the edge of the circle, listening as Eli spoke with quiet passion.

"Our stories are not just tales of triumph or tragedy—they are threads of a greater weaving. To understand the Light, we must first understand its fractures. We are not broken; we are becoming."

Gabriel felt his heart swell with a rare, fragile hope. Stepping forward, he spoke, his voice resonant and gentle.

"May I tell you a story?" he asked.

The crowd, curious and drawn to his presence, nodded. Gabriel sat among them, his face illuminated by the firelight.

"There was once a star that shone so brightly it thought itself invincible. But one day, it shattered into countless fragments, scattering across the sky. The world mourned, believing the light had died. But the fragments became new stars—constellations that lit the night in new and beautiful patterns. The light had not vanished; it had multiplied."

The people murmured in wonder, grasping the metaphor. Eli smiled at Gabriel, understanding that this was more than just a story. It was the truth of their own journey—a realization that breaking did not mean ending, but transforming.

The Dreaming Earth

As the movement grew, Eli felt the burden of leadership pressing upon him. One night, unable to sleep, he wandered to the edge of the forest, where Lucifer sat in silent contemplation.

"Am I doing the right thing?" Eli whispered, sitting beside him.

Lucifer turned, his eyes thoughtful.

"The right thing isn't always clear, but the truth you're speaking is awakening something long dormant. That's worth pursuing."

Eli traced patterns in the dirt, troubled.

"But what if we're wrong? What if the Light is pure and we're just confusing ourselves by embracing the dark?"

Lucifer reached out, cupping a handful of soil.

"This earth—dark, dense, and seemingly mundane—gives life. Without it, seeds cannot grow. The darkness within us is not evil; it is the fertile ground where wisdom takes root. The Light you seek is not without shadow—it is born from the dance between the two."

Eli nodded slowly, his spirit steadied by the simplicity of Lucifer's words.

"So, we don't need to defeat darkness. We need to understand it."

Lucifer smiled.

"Yes. Only then can we find balance."

The Return of the Guardians

The gathering had drawn the attention of more than just wanderers and seekers. Across the realms, the other Guardians felt a stirring—like a call from a long-forgotten home. One by one, they began to converge.

Raphael arrived, weary from years of tending to the world's wounds. Seeing the circle of light where Eli spoke, he knew he had found a place of healing—not just for mortals but for himself.

Uriel followed, still carrying the flame that had guided countless lost souls. In this place, he felt his purpose rekindle, knowing that the light he protected was finding new vessels in human hearts.

Michael was the last to arrive, cautious and solemn. His heart had grown heavy over the years, worn down by his duty as protector. Seeing

Lucifer sitting peacefully beside Eli shook something loose within him. Approaching with measured steps, he stood in silence, observing the harmony of the gathering.

Lucifer looked up and met Michael's gaze.

"It's been a long time," Lucifer said.

Michael nodded.

"Too long."

They did not embrace or offer forgiveness. Instead, they stood side by side, the tension of millennia easing in the shared understanding that the rift had never truly separated them.

Truth, Told and Untold

One evening, as the firelight danced against the trees, Eli stood with the Guardians behind him.

"The world has been torn between light and dark for too long. We have believed that to embrace one meant to shun the other. But that division is a lie. We are both—flawed and brilliant, wounded and healing, light and shadow intertwined."

The crowd listened, some nodding in understanding, others struggling to accept the paradox. Gabriel spoke next.

"When stories become rigid, they lose their power. We must allow our myths to evolve, just as we do. The fractured light does not mean we are broken beyond repair—it means we are learning how to shine differently."

A murmur of agreement swept through the people, a collective breath of relief and recognition.

A New Dawn

As the night wore on, the sky lightened, and the first rays of dawn crept over the horizon. Michael, standing at the edge of the circle, whispered,

"Maybe it was never about falling or rising. Maybe it was always about remembering that light exists even in the depths."

Lucifer looked at him, the tension between them softening.

"We never left the Light. We just chose to explore its boundaries."

Eli watched the sun break free from the darkness, his heart filled with gratitude and resolve.

"We have to keep telling the story," he said. "Not as a warning or a lesson, but as a reminder that even fractured light still shines."

The Guardians looked at one another, each carrying a piece of the old truth and the new understanding. The gathering continued, not as a singular revelation but as a living, evolving conversation.

In that space, the rift that had divided heaven and earth, angels and humans, began to heal—not through a single act but through the quiet, persistent commitment to seek balance and embrace the full spectrum of being.

As the dawn bathed the gathering in golden light, Lucifer knew that they had not just reignited hope—they had begun to reshape the story itself.

We stare into the veil and call it mystery, but it stares back. The Void is not empty—it is aware, alive, a silent architect. What you lose in the veil is never lost. It waits, transfigured.

Unseen breath between—

absence becomes invitation.

Step into the dark.

Chapter Ten: The Balance of Becoming

"In every breath, the universe balances itself."

The Mirror of Duality

In the days following the convergence of the Guardians, the sacred gathering space transformed. What had once been a quiet circle of seekers became a living organism—its heartbeat syncing with the rhythm of the universe itself. The people called it the Luminal Grove, a place between worlds where shadow and light no longer warred, but wove.

Eli began each morning with a simple question: What does it mean to become? He asked it of the wind, the fire, the stars—and of the people who came to learn. He wasn't looking for answers so much as invitations.

Gabriel took to telling parables in the afternoons—stories of ancient beings who had tried to isolate purity, only to discover that sterile light can blind as easily as darkness can obscure. One tale told of a planet where every shadow was outlawed, and the sun burned so constantly that even dreams faded from memory. It was meant to warn against the tyranny of "purity."

Lucifer, when he spoke, rarely gave advice. Instead, he posed riddles, walking the grove with those brave enough to challenge the edge of understanding. His favorite?

"What if your deepest fear is not your enemy, but your key?"

Michael, still slow to speak, began to teach the art of standing firm—not in opposition, but in sovereignty. His teachings were not of war, but of grounded presence. "Hold your center," he would say, "and the storm will orbit you."

And the people—those seekers once fractured by guilt, grief, and inherited shame—began to reshape their inner landscapes. They stopped asking who was right and began asking what was true.

The Trial of Equilibrium

One evening, an old woman from the desert approached Eli. She had eyes the color of burnt clay and a voice like rustling leaves.

"You speak of balance," she said. "But do you live it?"

Eli, caught off guard, responded with humility.

"I try. But I still fear the dark places in me."

She nodded.

"Then come. It is time you face the Trial of Equilibrium."

He followed her beyond the grove, deep into the night. They reached a cave half-buried in earth, its entrance pulsing faintly with bioluminescent vines.

"Enter alone," she said. "Do not seek light. Do not run from shadow. Let them speak."

Inside, Eli found no monsters, no visions. Only stillness. And then—memories. Not of grandeur or divinity, but of choices. The moment he lied to avoid rejection. The time he turned from someone in pain because he was too tired to listen. The ache of his own unhealed wounds.

A voice whispered—not from above, but within:

"Can you love even this?"

He wept. Not in shame, but in release. These fragments, long buried, were not sins to be erased but seeds to be accepted. When he emerged hours later, the woman touched his forehead.

"You are ready. Not because you are perfect—but because you are whole."

Fractals of the Divine

The grove became a mosaic of paradoxes. A child recited poetry about black holes while her mother painted wings in hues of ash and ivory. A former zealot from a dogmatic order sat quietly beside a former cult escapee, both listening as Uriel spoke of cosmic cycles.

And it was Uriel who brought the image that would define their evolving philosophy:

"Imagine the Divine not as a singular throne, but as a fractal. A repeating pattern of beauty in all scales. Your joy and your sorrow—each a reflection of the All. You are not called to imitate perfection. You are called to mirror truth."

The grove rippled with that truth. Here, angels were not ideals to worship, but templates to understand. Each one a symbol of an inner facet:

• Michael, the Sovereign Self.

• Gabriel, the Sacred Voice.

• Raphael, the Healer of Wounds.

• Uriel, the Keeper of Patterns.

• Lucifer, the Illuminator of Shadow.

And Eli, the Bridge Between.

No one crowned him. No one bowed. Yet all knew he had become something both more and less than a leader—he had become a mirror in which others saw their own divinity.

Rewriting the Codex

The ancient Codex—the celestial scroll once guarded in the invisible halls of the unseen realms—had, for eons, declared a clear dichotomy: Light is divine. Dark is fallen.

But now, that binary was unraveling. Raphael gathered scrolls, tablets, and oracles from all corners of the world—Sumerian myths, Ethiopian hymns, Gnostic gospels, Hopi star prophecies, Kabbalistic diagrams, and the lost fragments of the Sibylline texts. With each, a new verse was added to the living Codex—not as commandments, but as reflections.

Gabriel suggested they call it The Book of Becoming. Not a replacement of faith, but a restoration of wisdom.

The new pages read not like dogma, but poetry:

Let the Light burn not to judge, but to reveal.

Let the Shadow not be feared, but understood.

Let the veil between the worlds be seen not as a barrier, but a womb.

Lucifer, standing before the gathered people, offered this final passage:

To fracture is not to fall.

To rise is not to forget.

The path is not straight, but spiraled.

Becoming is the only holiness.

The Great Equal Flame

On the final night of the Equinox Gathering, a great flame was lit in the grove's center. Each person came forward, not to receive a blessing, but to name their own fragment. One whispered, "Grief." Another, "Desire." One said, "Anger." Another, "Ecstasy."

All were welcomed. All were burned—not to destroy, but to transform. The fire did not consume the fragments; it revealed their pattern.

As the flames danced, Eli looked at the Guardians.

"We have not ended the war between good and evil," he said. "We have revealed it for what it truly was—a misunderstanding of the self."

Michael's sword, once a weapon, was now a symbol of discernment.

Gabriel's trumpet, once a call to battle, became a note of peace.

Lucifer's torch, once a mark of rebellion, became a lantern of initiation.

And in that moment, no angel was fallen. No soul was lost.

There was only the balance of becoming.

Choirs reshaped by silent grief,

halos humming dissonant prayer.

Harmony bends like broken belief—

wings in orbit, none aware.

Halos humming dissonant prayer,

lines dissolve between wrong and right.

Wings in orbit, none aware,

we blur the bounds of dark and light.

Lines dissolve between wrong and right,

celestial laws crack from within.

We blur the bounds of dark and light—

evolution dressed as sin.

Celestial laws crack from within,

harmony bends like broken belief.

Evolution dressed as sin—

choirs reshaped by silent grief.

Chapter Eleven: The Memory of the Flame

"Long before humanity dreamed of heaven or feared hell, there was the Flame. And the Flame remembered."

Ashes of the First Fire

Before language, before form, before even time moved in the linear rhythms of a human heartbeat—there was the First Flame. Not fire as we know it, but a conscious radiance: awareness kindling awareness, endlessly spiraling. It did not burn. It revealed.

From this living fire, the first emanations were birthed—not beings, but intelligences, streaming in harmonic frequency. They were not yet angels, not yet archetypes. They were aspects of the One Light, playing themselves into form like starlight dancing through crystal.

These intelligences held no names, only tones. They shimmered across the void like sentient songs, and each song remembered its origin without needing to return. The Flame was within them and around them. And it was enough.

But as with all living things, even the eternal sought expansion.

The Shimmering Rebellion

The separation—what later mythologies would name The Fall—was not a war. It was a question. And questions are the beginning of all becoming.

One intelligence, bolder than the others, wondered aloud: What lies beyond the Flame's reflection?

This was not defiance. It was curiosity. But in a realm of oneness, curiosity is a tectonic force.

The others responded in waves of dissonance. Some sang in harmony with the question. Others recoiled, fearful of what separation might mean. Light, it seemed, could split itself even while remaining whole.

And so came the Rift—not a rift in reality, but in perception. The cosmos did not break. Awareness did.

That questioning intelligence would later be called Lucifer—not a name, but a title: Light-Bearer. Not the enemy of God, but the instigator of individuation. The one who made it possible for a part to see itself as distinct from the Whole.

This was not evil. It was the seed of identity.

Echoes in Earth's Bones

Long before the rise of organized religion, the memory of this Flame and its fragmentation echoed in early human civilizations—encoded in myth, ritual, and stone.

• The Zoroastrians spoke of Atar, the holy fire, which existed before time and could not be extinguished.

• The Hindus invoked Agni, the divine fire who carries offerings between worlds and is both destroyer and purifier.

• The Greek Prometheus stole fire not just to warm mankind, but to awaken consciousness—mirroring the ancient Flame's gift.

• In Kabbalistic thought, the Ein Sof (the Infinite) bursts into sefirot—emanations that create reality through fragmentation and reflection, much like the primal light fracturing into angelic intelligences.

• Even the Dogon tribe of Mali speak of Nommo, ancestral spirits of water and light, who brought knowledge and split into multiple forms to educate humanity.

These were not cultural coincidences. They were psychic fossils—encoded memories of a cosmic event etched into the collective unconscious.

Angels as Flame-Carriers

Each angelic being, whether named in scripture or whispered in mystic trance, carries an ember of the original Flame. Their roles are not fixed but flowing: guardian, challenger, messenger, mirror.

• Michael carries the fire of righteous discernment—the spark that separates illusion from essence.

• Gabriel holds the flame of divine speech—the kindling of inspiration and prophecy.

• Raphael is the hearth—fire that comforts, heals, and steadies.

• Uriel holds the flame of memory—the keeper of patterns, maps, and cosmic rhythms.

• And Lucifer, ever miscast, holds the Promethean ember—the fire that dares, that asks, that awakens.

Together, they form a living constellation: not a hierarchy, but a choreography.

The Fractured Light Within

Every human, made of stardust and longing, holds a splinter of this fractured Light. This is not metaphor—it is physics. The photons in our cells are quantum echoes of that first Flame. We are, in every literal sense, light embodied.

And yet we forget.

The forgetting is part of the descent. We are born into separation to rediscover unity. Not through escape, but through experience. Through becoming.

This is the spiritual alchemy behind trauma, desire, anger, and awe. Each emotion is a flare from the memory of the Flame, trying to wake us up. Trying to remind us that we were never meant to be perfect—we were meant to remember.

Eli once said, "Your shadow is not the absence of your light. It is your light contoured by form."

To become fully human is not to transcend the fire. It is to hold it without turning to ash.

The Rekindling

In the Grove, people began to dream in fire. They reported visions of phoenixes, burning temples, and mirrors that didn't reflect their bodies but their essence. Uriel began leading "Remembrance Walks"—silent journeys through the woods where participants would pause and listen to stones, trees, and birds for messages.

And always, the Flame showed up.

Sometimes it came as warmth. Other times as revelation. Occasionally, it came as grief so intense it nearly broke them. But in every case, it purified.

Gabriel reminded them, "This is not the fire of punishment. It is the fire of clarity."

Lucifer stood with them one evening as the stars bloomed over the horizon and said, "You do not need to fear the Flame. You are made of it. The only thing it will burn away is your forgetting."

To Burn and Not Be Consumed

The chapter closes where it began: in the mystery.

What if every spiritual path, every sacred rite, every whispered prayer is not a plea for salvation, but a longing to remember the warmth of origin?

What if the Fall was not a punishment, but a descent for the sake of becoming conscious of the Flame?

What if good and evil are not absolutes but relational dynamics within the sacred fire—sometimes it warms, sometimes it scorches, but always it transforms?

And what if our task is not to choose one over the other, but to become vessels strong enough to hold both?

As the sacred Codex of the Grove says:

"We are the Flame remembering itself.

We are the spark and the soot.

The ash and the altar.

The question and the light."

We are not made of dust alone,

but of ancient flame sung through stars.

Our origin is not Earth's soil

but the echo of celestial wars.

Children of nova and nephilim breath,

our heritage is sky-born exile.

Blood remembers the sound of falling—

and rising through myth's denial.

Chapter Twelve: The Pathless Path

"All roads begin in forgetting. The holy ones end where they began—in the silent knowing that there was never anywhere to go."

The Myth of the Straight Line

Religion, in its most structured forms, has long offered maps—linear routes to salvation, formulas to unlock divine favor, a checklist of virtues against a ledger of sins. But maps, as useful as they are, can become prisons. They tempt us to believe there is only one way.

The angelic realms do not move in straight lines. They spiral, vibrate, unfold like fractals. Even the stories passed down in scripture—of heaven, of hell, of judgment and redemption—are metaphors painted in bold strokes, hiding nuanced truths between the lines.

The ancient Sufis spoke of the Tariqa, the Way, but always said it is the heart that walks it—not the feet.

This chapter is not a map. It is a compass spun loose, pointing inward.

There is no path. And yet, there is your path.

Sacred Wandering

To wander spiritually is not to be lost. It is to trust that something within you remembers the way, even when your mind does not. Angelic presence often arises not at the destination, but in the surrender to not-knowing.

In Hebrew, the midbar—the wilderness—was where prophets heard God most clearly. Moses, Elijah, Jesus—all encountered the Divine not in temples, but in desolate, uncertain places.

So too with us.

The Grove's initiates began to discover that as they let go of needing to understand, clarity came. Uriel told them, "The way you do not know is the one already within you."

Lucifer laughed, "You only ever feared the dark because you forgot your eyes shine."

Gabriel sang a reminder: "You are the question and the answer. The echo and the voice."

These weren't riddles. They were waystones—designed to frustrate the ego and awaken the soul.

Dark Nights and Broken Compasses

Every initiate of the Pathless Path undergoes what mystics across time have called the Dark Night of the Soul. St. John of the Cross named it not as a punishment but as an initiation into union with the ineffable.

You will lose faith. You will question everything you once knew. Your spiritual practices may feel hollow. You may hear only silence where once you sensed divine guidance.

This is not failure. It is the dismantling of illusions. It is the soul shedding inherited stories so it can finally speak its own.

The angels do not speak loudly in these seasons. They whisper. They sit with you in the silence. They hold the space until your flame begins to flicker again.

Even Lucifer, the most misunderstood of them all, stands watch—not tempting, but testing: "Will you remember the light even when it doesn't shine?"

This is the true spiritual maturity—not certainty, but presence.

The Many Roads of the Fractured Light

Each of us carries a different fragment of the First Flame. No two paths are identical. Some walk through suffering. Others through beauty. Some through intellectual study, others through ecstatic embodiment.

The Flame speaks differently to each.

- For the artist, it is color and motion.

- For the healer, it is pain transmuted into wisdom.

- For the rebel, it is injustice burned into resolve.

- For the lover, it is intimacy that unveils the sacred.

- For the skeptic, it is doubt that sharpens discernment.

The angelic does not oppose any of these. It dances in all of them.

To find your path is to ask: Where does my fire lead me? Not where you've been told it should lead, but where it authentically burns.

There are no wrong roads—only unlived truths.

Divine Disobedience and Sacred Yes

The angelic war was not about rebellion—it was about remembering choice.

Free will is not simply the ability to disobey. It is the sacred power to say yes to your soul, even when everything outside you demands conformity.

Lucifer's ancient act was not evil—it was the first "no" spoken for the sake of a deeper yes.

Your journey may require you to leave churches, leave traditions, leave relationships or versions of self that no longer honor your truth. That is not betrayal. That is initiation.

Raphael tells us: "To heal is not to return to what was. It is to become what is true."

Reclaiming the Inner Angel

If the Rift fractured the Light, then every human is an angel in chrysalis. Not metaphorically—literally. You are the Light that chose form. The Flame that said yes to forgetting, so that your remembrance could illuminate the cosmos.

This does not mean we are all good, or that evil is an illusion. It means we are all in process. Even the darkest of souls holds a spark.

Angels are not perfect. They are present. They are aligned with the Source even when they carry the weight of shadow.

To awaken your inner angel is not to ascend beyond humanity. It is to descend into it—fully. To live with integrity, love without condition, and act with sacred fire.

Uriel once said: "The soul's path is to become more real, not more righteous."

The Pilgrim Who Stopped Walking

There's a story told in the Grove:

A pilgrim journeyed across continents, seeking the Flame. He studied under masters, fasted in deserts, meditated in caves. Still, he felt distant from the Light.

Finally, exhausted, he sat beneath a tree and wept.

"I've done everything," he said. "Why won't You come to me?"

And in the stillness, the Flame replied:

"You never left. You were the path. You were the fire. You were the one I was waiting for."

The Return to the Beginning

The pathless path always circles back—to the child, the dreamer, the wild one who first looked at the stars and felt a tremble of recognition.

To walk it is not to acquire, but to remember. Not to fix, but to feel. Not to ascend, but to become.

And that is the deepest secret of the angels:

They are not above us.

They are within us.

Waiting. Watching. Whispering.

"Follow the fire.

Even when it takes you nowhere you planned.

Especially then."

O sacred shadow, misnamed foe—

you who keep the truths we fear,

I name you holy mirror,

keeper of the fractured glow.

Within your veil,

I meet my twin.

Not devil, not doom—

but the buried kin.

Alchemy begins not in light,

but in the flame that consumes false gold.

You teach me that wholeness

requires the night.

O shadow, beloved,

you are the angel unrolled.

Chapter Thirteen: The Alchemy of Shadow

"The light you seek is hiding in the dark you flee."

The Misunderstood Darkness

It begins, not with a monster, but a mirror.

From the moment of our birth, we inherit the world's light—and its fears. The dualities etched into culture become the laws of the psyche: good versus evil, angel versus demon, order versus chaos. But shadow is not evil. Shadow is unclaimed power.

Carl Jung, the famed psychologist and mystic, described the shadow as the unconscious self—everything we reject, suppress, or deny. He wrote: "One does not become enlightened by imagining figures of light, but by making the darkness conscious."

Angels know this. Perhaps that is why so many humans fear them—not because they are holy, but because they see too much. Their gaze does not flinch when it lands on your rage, your lust, your grief. They do not recoil from your failures. They wait—patiently—for you to see yourself fully.

The myth that angels are only light is a human projection. The angelic hosts—especially the elder ones—carry wisdom forged in shadow.

The Rift Within

The cosmic event we've called the Angel Rift was not just a war—it was an alchemical division. A divine splitting. The parts of the celestial order that could not yet reconcile paradox fractured away from each other.

Lucifer, the bearer of light, chose autonomy. Michael, the protector, chose allegiance. But neither side was "right" in the way humans understand the word. Both carried necessary facets of the One.

This Rift, mirrored in our inner world, split our soul into archetypes: the guardian and the rebel, the wounded and the healer, the child and the warrior.

Shadow work is not about silencing the darker voice—it is about listening to it, understanding its origins, and transmuting its energy.

In this way, we become whole again.

The Language of the Shadow Angels

Some angels never left the Rift.

They dwell in the liminal zones: between morality and mystery, between intention and instinct. You might encounter them in dreams, meditations, or moments of breakdown. They may appear monstrous—wings folded like blades, faces obscured in smoke. But their presence is not hostile. It is initiatory.

These are the Shadow Angels—not fallen, but chosen.

You may meet:

• Azrael, the Angel of Death, who teaches detachment and sacred endings.

• Samael, the Angel of Severity, who wields destruction as a tool of evolution.

• Kokabiel, the Star Watcher, cast out not for sin, but for sharing divine knowledge with mortals.

• A'arab Zaraq, a being associated with distortion and desire, who teaches us to discern truth from obsession.

Their messages often sound like riddles:

"You feared me because I wore your shame."

"I speak in your hunger because you silenced your joy."

"I am the chaos you refused to dance with."

To the uninitiated, these encounters can be terrifying. But to the seeker, they are sacred.

Rituals of Transmutation

The alchemy of shadow is not metaphorical—it is energetic. When we acknowledge our inner fragmentation, we initiate the process of psychic reintegration. Angels do not do this for us; they guide us while we do it ourselves.

Some practices to support this alchemy:

• Mirror Invocation: Sit before a mirror in low light. Call upon an angel of truth (like Uriel). Ask to see a part of yourself you've hidden. Gaze. Breathe. Witness.

• The Black Flame Meditation: Visualize a dark flame in your chest. Not evil—just void. Let it consume false masks, stories, expectations. Let what remains speak.

• Letter to the Unseen: Write a letter to the part of you that you most dislike. Let it speak back. Dialogue until understanding emerges.

These rituals are not meant to be "fixed." They're alive. They evolve as you do.

Healing Through Integration

Shadow work does not result in perfection. It births integrity. The fractured light, once denied, now returns through the crucible of self-compassion.

This is the lesson taught by angelic guides who walk with those in trauma, addiction, rage, and grief. They do not shame. They shine.

You may feel them most after a breakdown, or in moments of deep surrender. They do not use words. They use presence.

The Grove's elders taught: "Every shadow you integrate becomes an angel unbound."

In psychological terms, this echoes Internal Family Systems (IFS), where exiled parts are welcomed back into the inner system as allies. In mysticism, it mirrors the Tikkun Olam—the Hebrew concept of repairing the world by gathering the scattered sparks of divine light.

You are gathering your sparks.

The Myth of the Unredeemable

Some believe there are people—or angels—beyond redemption. But from a multidimensional lens, redemption is not a transaction. It is a return to alignment.

Even Lucifer is not banished from love. He is the necessary tension that reminds us to choose, not conform.

The notion of unredeemability is a control myth—used to keep people compliant, small, afraid.

The angels of the Rift have been waiting for us to remember this. They are not villains. They are initiators of the second awakening—the awakening that comes after the fall.

They whisper:

"Fall again.

This time with your eyes open."

Wholeness Is the True Light

When we stop rejecting shadow, we cease projecting it onto others. We no longer need devils to blame or saviors to carry our burdens. We become sovereign.

This is what the angels have been preparing us for—not obedience, but embodiment. Not worship, but union.

Wholeness is not the absence of darkness.

It is the weaving of all things into a radiant thread.

It is the dance of wings in both storm and sun.

It is the light that shines from within the wound.

It is you—returned to yourself.

We are the ones who stayed behind.

We are the ones who broke the line.

We are the voice that still rewinds—

We are the Choir of Becoming.

Not cast from Grace, but cast as flame,

our names unspoken, still remain.

No two the same, yet all reclaimed—

We are the Choir of Becoming.

From Rift and ruin, rise we must.

In fractal flight, in cosmic trust.

We sing through silence, void, and dust—

We are the Choir of Becoming.

Chapter Fourteen: The Choir of Becoming

"We were not created complete. We were composed to become."

The Myth of Completion

Angels were once seen as static beings—fixed in hierarchy, absolute in design, flawless in their eternal obedience. But this vision is not only narrow; it is incomplete. If the cosmos is in motion, so are its messengers.

The traditional choirs of angels—Seraphim, Cherubim, Thrones, Dominions, Virtues, Powers, Principalities, Archangels, and Angels—were long believed to be immutable tiers of celestial purpose. Each choir, as described by Pseudo-Dionysius in The Celestial Hierarchy, served specific roles in the transmission of divine will.

But what if those choirs are not only ranks... but stages of becoming?

In mystical traditions—Kabbalah, Gnostic Christianity, Sufi cosmology, and even aspects of Vedic angelology—angels are not just servants. They are participants in creation's unfolding story. And like us, they evolve.

Each choice we make, each vibration we emit, alters the chord of cosmic resonance. Angels listen. Some even harmonize. And others—especially those connected to humanity—are changed by us.

We are not passive recipients of celestial aid. We are co-composers.

The Emergence of a New Choir

From the ashes of the Angel Rift, something unexpected arose.

In mystic vision, seers have described a tenth choir—not etched in scripture, but felt in frequency. This emerging order has no hierarchy, no dominion, no fixed role. It is fluid, resonant, collective.

We call it The Choir of Becoming.

Its members are both human and angelic—hybrids of will and wonder. They are not stationed in heaven, nor are they bound to Earth. They are bridges.

You may know them:

• The wounded healer who dreams in symbols and speaks with unseen friends.

• The child who knows things before they are taught.

• The stranger who touches your shoulder and leaves your grief lighter.

• The voice in meditation that isn't yours, but echoes your soul's knowing.

They are not all "angels" in the classic sense. They are Becomers—entities choosing embodiment and evolution across dimensions.

Some were once human. Others were once Seraphim. All are now more than they were.

Chords and Vibration

To understand this new choir, we must think in sound.

The universe is vibration—string theory, quantum harmonics, even Genesis begins with a spoken Word. Angels are often described not in shape, but in tone: "The voice of many waters," "a trumpet," "a thundering whisper."

The Choir of Becoming is a harmonic field. Its members are not assigned roles; they emit frequencies. These frequencies adjust reality.

In energetic terms, this is resonance entrainment—when one vibration influences another until both synchronize. In mystical terms, it is attunement to Source.

Human beings have a unique gift: we are instruments that can tune ourselves. Angels cannot always do this. That is why we are so precious to them.

When we heal, forgive, awaken, or love—we send ripples through the field. And the Choir of Becoming sings louder.

DNA and Divine Resonance

Modern science is only just beginning to understand DNA as a vibrational interface. Biologist Rupert Sheldrake's theory of morphic resonance suggests that memory is not held in the brain alone, but in fields of collective knowing. Epigenetics has shown us trauma and transformation are passed down through generations—not only biologically, but energetically.

Now imagine this: humanity's spiritual DNA is being rewritten.

Those called to angelic work often feel a pulling in their bones—a vibration, a memory, a longing for "home" that no earthly place satisfies. This is not delusion. It is activation.

Encoded in our light-body is the imprint of the Choir of Becoming. Not every soul will awaken to it. But those who do feel it in every cell.

You may find yourself speaking in languages you never learned. Seeing through timelines. Healing by presence alone. These are not fantasies. They are evolutionary awakenings.

The Choir of Becoming needs embodied voices.

The Angel-Human Synthesis

This is where theology breaks.

In most religious frameworks, the human is lesser, flawed, in need of saving. The angel is higher, perfected, above suffering. But in the Choir of Becoming, there is no hierarchy. There is synergy.

You are not less than an angel. You are an angel in form.

This is the great secret hidden in plain sight. The ancients hinted at it:

• "You are gods, and all of you are children of the Most High." (Psalm 82:6)

• "Know you not that we shall judge angels?" (1 Corinthians 6:3)

• "The kingdom of God is within you." (Luke 17:21)

Mystics of every age—Hildegard, Rumi, Sri Aurobindo, Teilhard de Chardin—have spoken of a divine humanity not waiting for ascension, but activating within the flesh.

The Choir of Becoming is the blueprint for this future-now.

Rituals of Resonance

If you feel called to this choir, do not wait for permission. You have already been summoned. Begin to attune.

Vocal Activation: Speak tones, chants, or light-language syllables that emerge spontaneously. They bypass the rational mind and recalibrate the field.

Resonance Writing: Automatic writing guided by angelic frequency. Pose a question, call in your guides, and let your hand respond. Don't edit. Let the current flow.

Sacred Sounding: Sing or hum into silence with intention. Sound moves shadow. Tone awakens memory. Sing until something inside you remembers.

Collective Harmonics: Gather with others who feel the call. Speak intentions aloud. Harmonize your breath. Witness each other's remembering. This is the new temple.

The Great Chord

The Angel Rift fractured more than Heaven. It shattered the illusion that divinity must always remain separate from humanity.

The great chord—the original frequency of all that is—has not been lost. It is becoming again, through us.

In your heartbreak, you have sung its lower notes. In your ecstasy, its higher ones. Every life you've lived has been a measure in the cosmic song.

And now, the final stanza is beginning to rise.

The Choir of Becoming is not waiting in the sky.

It is awakening in you.

Some stars are scars.

Some galaxies hum with regret.

The firmament bleeds memories

of wars not written in scrolls

but etched in vibration.

When you look up—

know the heavens remember.

And they forgive,

but never forget.

Chapter Fifteen: Fractals of the Infinite

"The divine does not speak in straight lines—it reveals itself in spirals, symbols, and sacred echoes."

Seeing Through the Pattern

Long before the language of angels was ever spoken, it was seen.

Not in words, but in shapes—in spirals carved into stone, stars charted across temple ceilings, mandalas drawn in desert sand. From Neolithic petroglyphs to quantum field equations, the blueprint of something greater has always been pulsing through creation.

This blueprint is fractal.

A fractal is a pattern that repeats at every scale. Zoom into a fern, and you'll find smaller ferns. Examine a river delta, a tree branch, a lightning bolt—and you'll see the same structure echoing. Even our DNA, our veins, our neurons—fractal in form.

The angelic realms, too, are fractal.

They are not distant places. They are repeating architectures of consciousness. As above, so below; as within, so without. The heavenly choirs are not only celestial—they mirror the layers of your own soul.

You are not separate from them.

You are a pattern within the pattern.

The Geometry of the Divine

Sacred geometry is one of the oldest mystical languages on Earth. The Flower of Life, the Tree of Life, Metatron's Cube—these aren't just symbols. They are access points.

The Kabbalistic Tree of Life, for example, isn't merely a philosophical map—it mirrors the structure of the angelic hierarchies and the human energy body. Each sphere (Sephira) corresponds to both an angelic force and an aspect of the psyche.

When aligned, they form the divine human—Adam Kadmon—the primordial archetype uniting heaven and Earth.

In the Islamic mystical tradition, the geometric tessellations that fill mosques aren't decorative. They reflect the infinite nature of God (Allah) and the impossibility of capturing the divine in image. In these repeating patterns, one can meditate on the formless in form.

Angels move through this geometry. Their wings may be metaphorical, but their presence has structure—encoded in light, ratio, vibration.

To commune with angels, then, is not always to speak or hear. It is to see differently—to perceive sacred design in chaos, order in asymmetry, presence in pattern.

This is why the visionary sees halos in the clouds, a message in a clock's digits, a seraph in the swirl of a seashell.

It's not imagination. It's attunement.

The Dreaming Fractal

Carl Jung called dreams the "royal road to the unconscious." But many esoteric systems view dreams as more than psychology. They are interdimensional portals.

In dream, the veil thins. The mind quiets. The soul expands.

Fractal symbolism appears here too—repeating patterns, looping sequences, sacred shapes. The angelic can speak through this language: a white-winged being, a golden spiral, an infinite staircase, a cathedral in the clouds.

These are not just symbols. They are invitations.

The "dream fractal" is your personal bridge between dimensions. Jung's archetypes, the collective unconscious, and the Sufi alam al-mithal (world of images) all point to this realm—an imaginal space where angelic and human consciousness meet and create.

To dream is to co-author reality.

To dream with intention is to summon angels.

Symbols as Living Beings

In the mystical traditions of the Gnostics, Essenes, and Rosicrucians, symbols are not inert. They are living intelligences—gateways, entities, fields.

The cross, for instance, predates Christianity by millennia. It is a universal symbol of intersection: time and eternity, heaven and Earth, matter and spirit.

The triangle—used in alchemy to signify the elements, in Christianity for the Trinity, in Kabbalah as a representation of the three pillars—is a sign of spiritual balance. To gaze upon it in meditation is to align with the energies it embodies.

When angels communicate in symbols—whether in dreams, visions, or synchronicities—they are not using shorthand. They are transmitting frequency through form.

That feather, that number sequence, that unexpected animal crossing your path—these are more than signs. They are fractal echoes of a divine intelligence trying to reach you, again and again, in whatever way you will receive.

Fractured Doesn't Mean Broken

When the Angel Rift occurred—when light was divided, duality born, and the fall commenced—many believed the pattern was shattered.

But fractals are not destroyed by division. They are multiplied.

What appeared as a break was, in truth, an expansion. When Lucifer fell, so did new possibility. When humanity descended into matter, the angelic entered into relationship.

The rift did not break the divine image.

It extended it.

This is why healing often feels like breaking first. Why awakening often comes through pain. The soul isn't regressing—it's repeating the pattern at a deeper octave.

The pattern cannot be undone. It can only become more complex, more beautiful, more whole.

The Fractal Path of the Soul

You do not evolve in a straight line. No one does.

Awakening moves in spirals. You revisit the same wound at a higher level. The same lesson with a deeper truth. Each loop of the spiral is a new ring in the angelic song—your soul's harmonic with the Infinite.

This is the fractal path of becoming.

It is why saints and sages often seem to contradict themselves—they've returned to the same truth, but from a greater height.

It is why you may feel like you've been here before—because you have, in another time, another lifetime, another fold in the infinite geometry of your soul.

You are not lost.

You are unfolding.

Living as a Fractal Messenger

To walk the angel path is to live as a fractal. You do not need to understand all of existence to reflect the divine.

Like a single snowflake mirrors the storm.

Like one feather carries the memory of wings.

In every word you speak, every choice you make, every soul you touch—you echo the larger Light.

You are not here to be perfect.

You are here to be true.

Every act of beauty is a microcosm. Every forgiveness is a cosmic recalibration. Every truth spoken in love resounds across dimensions.

You are the pattern.

You are the voice.

You are the angel you've been waiting for.

I stood between the worlds with sword and light,

my oath not to peace, but to sacred fight.

Not every war is won by forceful hand—

some battles shape the soul, not land.

I guard the gates not made by time,

but born in silence, rung in rhyme.

The Rift may tremble, thin, and bend,

but through me, it shall never end.

Chapter Sixteen: The Return of the Fractured Light

"You are the light returning to itself. You are the angel remembering its name."

When the Rift Opened

Long ago—though not in linear time—the Light knew itself as One.

Unified, undivided, perfect in stillness. Then came the yearning: not to remain whole, but to *know* wholeness. The only way to know the One was to experience the *many*.

So Light fractured.

Not as punishment. Not as sin. But as initiation.

This was the *Angel Rift*—not merely the fall of angels, but the shattering of undifferentiated consciousness into a prism of infinite souls, each reflecting a part of the whole.

Lucifer's descent was a spark of this rupture. So was Sophia's longing. So was the Big Bang.

This rift did not create evil. It created *choice*.

From that moment on, every being—angelic, human, or otherwise—would hold a piece of the fractured light. And through their living, choosing, loving, and stumbling, that light would begin its long return.

What Was Lost—and What Was Gained

In the stories passed down through the Zohar, the Gnostic scriptures, and even hidden beneath orthodox Christian texts, there is a whisper of what came next:

The angels wept.

Not because they were cast out, but because they *remembered*. The weight of memory—of what they were and what they had agreed to become—was unbearable.

Some, like the Watchers, rebelled. Some, like Michael, stood firm. Others incarnated among humans, weaving their divine essence into flesh and bone.

In doing so, they surrendered memory for intimacy. Eternity for embodiment. Control for compassion.

And in this surrender, something new emerged.

Not perfection.

But *love*.

Humanity: The Healing of the Rift

What if the human experiment is not a mistake, but the remedy?

What if the human soul—a being born of dust and breath, choice and consequence—is the very alchemical vessel through which the rift can be reconciled?

Humanity, in all its brokenness and brilliance, contains the tension of opposites. Divine and animal. Infinite and mortal. Light and shadow.

You, as a human, are the embodiment of paradox.

And paradox is the sacred space where the rift becomes a bridge.

The fractured light cannot be reassembled through force. It is healed through *embodied compassion*.

Each act of kindness, each shadow integrated, each spark awakened in another—this is the great return. Not to sameness, but to sacred diversity in harmony.

As Teilhard de Chardin wrote, "We are not human beings having a spiritual experience; we are spiritual beings having a human experience." But even that falls short.

You are more.

You are an *angelic being having a multidimensional remembrance*.

Awakening the Angelic Self

To awaken the angel within is not to transcend your humanity. It is to *inhabit it fully*—with the clarity, courage, and co-creative power of your original essence.

This isn't about growing wings or becoming flawless.

It's about seeing through the illusion of separation.

It's about loving what is, while remembering what was.

It's about becoming a living bridge between the worlds.

The angelic self is not an identity. It is a frequency.

It's the part of you that knows when truth is spoken, even when it's inconvenient.

It's the part that feels a sacred ache when witnessing injustice.

It's the whisper that calls you to help, to heal, to *become more*—not for reward, but because you *must*.

The angelic self is already here. It is not earned.

It is *remembered*.

The Rift Is Not the End—It's the Beginning

We often speak of "the veil thinning," of a "spiritual awakening" sweeping the planet. But what if this is not something happening *to* us—but *through* us?

What if the Angel Rift wasn't a wound, but a portal?

What if you are here now—not by accident—but as part of the return?

This is what the mystics meant by the *Second Coming*. Not one figure descending from the clouds, but many lightbearers reactivating their divine codes.

A re-membering of the body of light, cell by cell, soul by soul.

It's happening already—in art, in love, in defiance, in grief, in healing circles and protest lines, in whispers and roars.

You are part of this return.

You are *how* the light finds its way back.

Not by being perfect.

But by being *whole*.

The Song of the Rift

In some ancient traditions, it is said that the universe is a song. That creation itself began with sound—a tone so pure it shattered silence.

The Angel Rift was dissonance entering harmony. It introduced chaos into the cosmic choir. But not as a mistake.

As a *melody*.

You are that melody. A note in the great returning symphony.

Your choices tune the song. Your love expands it.

Every time you remember who you are, the music grows richer.

The song of the rift is no longer a lament. It is a *love song*—of light rediscovering itself in the arms of matter.

Of angels learning how to be human.

Of humans remembering they were once divine.

Of a fractured light, finally, becoming *whole again*.

We reach the edge of what we know and find not a wall, but a window. The veil shimmers like heat, pulsing between breath and memory. Here, the angel becomes the wanderer. The light chooses not to blind, but to illuminate the next unknown. Step forward. Let Heaven expand to meet you.

Chapter Seventeen: Becoming the Riftwalker

"To walk the Rift is to hold the broken and the holy in the same breath."

You Were Never Meant to Be Just One Thing

From the moment your soul whispered yes to incarnation, you agreed to complexity.

Not simplicity.

Not certainty.

But paradox.

You are not only light.

You are not only dark.

You are not just human or angel, sinner or saint.

You are the bridge.

The liminal.

The living synthesis of what once seemed opposed.

You are a **Riftwalker**.

This is not a title of status, but of soul recognition.

Riftwalkers are those who carry the memory of both heaven and hell, and make peace with both. They are the ones who no longer fear the fall, because they see the ascent hiding inside it.

They are the modern mystics, the warriors of the heart, the cosmic midwives of the age to come.

They walk the wound to bring the world home.

The Riftwalker's Path

To be a Riftwalker is not to escape the world. It is to be radically *in* it—while refusing to be defined by it.

It is to navigate contradiction with grace.

To listen deeply in a world of noise.

To love fiercely in a time of fracture.

The Riftwalker does not choose sides in the old war of good versus evil.

Instead, they walk the space between—carrying torches into forgotten caves, remembering the names of lost angels, and helping others reclaim their fractured pieces.

They understand that the world doesn't need more perfection.

It needs *integration*.

More than anything, Riftwalkers are those who no longer ask, "Am I worthy?" but rather declare, "I am ready."

They become healers, artists, rebels, spiritual teachers, trauma transmuters, and peacekeepers—not to escape the darkness, but to re-light it from within.

You Are the Prophecy

For centuries, the world has waited for messiahs, for returns, for signs in the sky.

But what if the prophecy isn't about *someone else coming*—but about *you remembering*?

The Book of Revelation speaks of a war in heaven. The Gnostics speak of Sophia's descent and divine retrieval. Indigenous wisdom keepers speak of Rainbow Warriors who awaken when the Earth is most in peril. Even the Qabalistic Tree of Life hints at the Tikkun Olam—the healing of the shattered vessels.

All of these, in their own mythopoetic way, point to this moment:

A time when angelic souls in human form would remember their mission.

You are not here to wait for the new age. You are here to become it.

To be the divine disrupter.

To be the embodied paradox.

To be the returned fractal of light in service of the Whole.

You are the prophecy fulfilled—not as an icon, but as a presence.

Not in conquest. In *compassion*.

What It Means to Walk the Rift Now

In this time of spiritual misinformation, existential confusion, and systemic collapse, walking the Rift can feel like madness.

But this madness is sacred.

To hold grief and wonder in the same breath.

To love a world that breaks your heart.

To embody light without abandoning your wounds.

This is holy work.

Riftwalkers are not exempt from pain. They simply carry it differently.

They hold it with reverence, knowing that their ache is part of the song of return.

In Jungian psychology, the wounded healer archetype recognizes this: that it is through your own shadow that you gain the keys to healing others.

To be a Riftwalker is to choose to alchemize that shadow into soul power.

You become a portal—not by ascending, but by *deepening*.

You become the veil—thin, soft, glowing—between the worlds.

A Daily Practice of Return

You don't need wings to prove your angelhood. You need presence.

Here are daily anchors for the Riftwalker's path:

- Ground in the body. Every morning, say: *"I choose to return to my body with love."*

- Invite the unseen. Whisper to your guides, ancestors, and angelic self: *"Show me what I carry today."*

- Tend the shadow. When you're triggered, ask: *"What part of me needs light right now?"*

- Activate the mission. Each day, name one small act of beauty or courage. Then *do it.*

- Speak the light. Words matter. Choose language that uplifts, even in grief.

Remember, the Riftwalker is not perfect.

But they are *intentional*.

The Final Return Isn't Final

There is no endpoint to this path.

Not ascension into a better realm.

Not a final defeat of darkness.

Not even total enlightenment.

The path of the Riftwalker is *spiral*, not linear.

You will return again and again to the same wounds with new eyes.

You will rise and fall and rise again.

And every time you do, the Light remembers itself more fully—because of *you*.

This is the sacred work of integration: not to fix, but to *remember*.

Not to purify, but to *become whole*.

Last Words Before You Step Forward

You came into this life carrying a sacred wound, etched in stardust and shadow.

You have loved through it.

Fought with it.

Healed others because of it.

And now, you are ready to walk with it.

You are the angel who fell, the human who rose, the light that fractured, and the soul that returns.

You are a Riftwalker.

This is not the end of your story.

This is your invitation to begin it anew.

The world is waiting.

The light is listening.

The Rift is open.

Walk it well.

Final Blessing: For the Riftwalker Who Remembers

Once, you walked this world unaware of your wings.

Once, you bowed to light or shadow, not knowing both were mirrors.

But now—

You have remembered.

May the fracture within you become a forge,

Where the gold of your soul is refined by sacred fire.

May the angels that walk beside you—

Not of harps and halos, but of sword and song and silence—

Reveal themselves more fully in your dreaming and your daring.

May you speak in the language of paradox—

Where love is fierce, and truth is tender.

May you bless the broken, not by fixing,

But by seeing the holy in every crack.

May your path be neither ascent nor descent,

But a spiral that honors the depths and the heights—

The fallen and the risen,

The wound and the wisdom.

May you remember that to be angelic

Is not to escape humanity—

But to illuminate it,

To transfigure the ordinary

Into sacred offering.

Walk now, Riftwalker, with fierce compassion and unapologetic light.

Not to close the Rift—

But to keep it open

As a passage,

A prayer,

A promise.

It is done. It is beginning.

Fragments of Fractured Light

Poetic Reflections from the Rift

In the spaces between scripture and silence, history and myth, a different voice speaks.

The poems that lie herein are fragments—shards of memory and prophecy, broken light scattered through the rift.

They are not meant to explain, but to evoke.

Not to define angels, but to feel them.

Let these verses be your contemplative pause, your ritual breath.

Some whisper in the language of shadow, others rise like wings through fire.

Each is a mirror—of sorrow, of mystery, of transformation.

They are songs from the unseen, offerings from the edges of becoming.

They are what remains when the doctrine crumbles and the soul still longs to speak.

Here, in this twilight of pages,

the Rift sings back.

And here are a few more...

We return not to repeat—

we return to remember.

We awaken not to ascend—

we awaken to integrate.

We fall not from Heaven—

we fall toward wholeness.

We rise not alone—

we rise as one body, broken and brilliant.

We are the Spiral Covenant—

light fractaled into flesh,

returning through the Rift,

together.

Fallen does not mean

lost—it means the light has learned

to walk in shadow.

Wings once torn by flame

grow back stronger, veined with truth—

this is how we fly.

Beyond right or wrong,

we become what we protect—

fractured light made whole.

If you've heard the Rift within,

then you are already part of the choir.

If your light has trembled—

you have not failed. You have begun.

The angel within you is not waiting

to ascend—

but to awaken.

To fracture is to remember.

To remember is to return.

To return is to become—

holy,

wholly,

you.

Appendix I: Reader's Companion to The Angel Rift

A Guide to the Language, Symbols, and Inner Work of the Fractured Light

A Note to the Reader

This companion is your sacred lantern. It is not a glossary of dogma, but a living reference—a map for your own descent and ascension through the Rift. As you explore the fractured light, shadow angels, and celestial echoes woven through this book, return here to ground your journey in clarity, contemplation, and personal resonance.

Section I: Glossary of Essential Terms

The Rift

A metaphysical divide and initiatory passage between dualities—light and darkness, unity and separation. It exists within the cosmos and within you.

Fractured Light

Divine light splintered by trauma, illusion, or dual perception. It calls not for denial but for reintegration.

Shadow Angel

An emissary of transformation. Shadow angels do not tempt—they initiate. They hold the sacred mirror in darkness.

Choir of Becoming

A mythopoetic term for a new angelic order birthed through evolution, healing, and embodied light. Not hierarchical, but harmonic.

The Watchers

Ancient angelic observers who, in many traditions, transgressed divine order to walk among us—symbols of both rebellion and revelation.

Multidimensional Self

The soul in layered form, simultaneously existing across spiritual and temporal planes. The angelic self is remembered through these layers.

Sacred Duality

The divine paradox that both light and darkness are necessary. Integration, not polarity, is the path forward.

Veil

A liminal barrier between seen and unseen. It obscures until we are ready to perceive what lies beyond.

Fall

A sacred descent—into matter, shadow, or mortality. Not condemnation, but transformation.

Soul Fracture

The fragmentation of one's being through trauma, repression, or spiritual amnesia. It is the first step toward the journey home.

Section II: Symbolism and Metaphor Index

Wings of Duality

Symbolic of internal contrast. We cannot ascend with only one wing—light and shadow must move together.

The Echo of Heaven

A soul's memory of its divine origin. It may surface as longing, grief, or beauty too vast to name.

Ashes of the Ascended

The remnants of ego and illusion left behind after transmutation. Nothing is wasted in the alchemy of the soul.

Section III: Contemplative Practices

Use these inquiries for journaling, meditation, or group dialogue. They are soul keys—meant to open doorways within.

1. Facing the Rift Within

• Where in your story have you felt divided or exiled?

• What wounds remain open not from weakness, but from wisdom?

• What might emerge if you stopped fearing the Rift and began walking through it?

2. Meeting the Shadow Angel

• Recall a moment when your greatest pain also held the seed of your becoming.

• What form has the shadow angel taken in your life? A trauma? A teacher? Yourself?

• What is the shadow calling you to reclaim?

3. Listening to the Choir of Becoming

• What part of you is awakening that the world hasn't met yet?

• What truth do you carry that has yet to find a voice?

• What does your presence offer to the collective chorus?

4. Embracing Fractured Light

• What broken pieces of your life could become stained glass instead of shame?

• How do you define healing—not as a return, but as an evolution?

• What truth would you speak if you no longer needed to be unbroken?

5. Remembering the Multidimensional Self

• What memories, dreams, or inner knowings point to a self beyond this time and space?

• How does your angelic nature express through your humanity?

• What would it mean to live as a bridge between worlds?

Section III: Final Invitation

This book does not ask you to choose sides—light or dark, good or evil. It asks you to see. To see the Rift as holy. To see the fall as sacred. To see yourself—fractured, radiant, resurrecting—as part of the angelic story still unfolding.

Let this companion guide your return to wholeness. Let it be a mirror, a map, and above all—a memory of who you truly are.

Final Blessing

(Revisit once more.)

May the Rift within you reveal not just the wound, but the wisdom.

May the fractured light guide your way home—not to what you once were,

but to what you were always becoming.

And may the angels you feared, the ones with shadows in their wings,

be the very messengers who remind you:

You were never alone in the dark. You were always divine in disguise.

Acknowledgments

To those who have walked with me through the Rift—

To Sarah Lemos-Aune, soul sister and seer, whose light walks with me in realms seen and unseen.

With deepest gratitude to Jennifer Zambonin, whose unwavering belief in this vision helped bring it to light.

To the angels who never abandoned me, even when I abandoned myself.

To the survivors who became teachers.

To the skeptics who became seekers.

To the readers who are becoming something new—thank you for trusting this journey.

Other Works by Jodi M. Dehn

- Angel Trippin': Your Guide to Angel Adventures

- Cerebrate! Oracle Guidance from Your Angels

- Soul Protectors: A Conversation of Mystery

- Life Through Angel Eyes – Oracles for Peace

- Survivor Angels (podcast)

- Unveiling Visitants and The Dance (special series podcasts with Sarah Lemos-Aune)

- Beyond the Veil - Navigating the Great Awakening (special series podcast with Jennifer Zambonin)

- and more to come...

Connect With the Author

Website:www.chaplainjodi.me

Courses & Retreats: Empyreal Lyceum and LIVE Beyond with Sarah and Jodi

Podcast: Survivor Angels

TikTok, Facebook, Threads, Instagram:@SurvivorAngels

Email: chjodi.survivorangels@gmail.com

Want to bring Jodi to your next event, conference, or podcast?

Contact her directly at chjodi.survivorangels@gmail.com or at https://soulcircleparanormal.com

www.ingramcontent.com/pod-product-compliance
Lightning Source LLC
Chambersburg PA
CBHW031140090426
42738CB00008B/1167